It's No Picnic For Me Either Buster

Illustrations by Citicia Smith

Story by Adele McCurdy and Alan Woods

For information regarding permission, write to:
Cookietown Inc.
PO Box 360586
Columbus, Ohio 43236-0586

Visit our website at **www.cookietownworld.com**

It's No Picnic For Me Either Buster
Illustrations by Citicia Smith
Story by Adele McCurdy and Alan Woods

Summary: Ms. Sugar the schoolteacher helps one student learn the rewards of studying and hard work.
1. Cookietown—Fiction, 2. Cookies—Fiction

ISBN: 978-0-9818477-0-2

Manufactured by:
BookMasters, Inc.
30 Amberwood Parkway
Ashland, OH 44805
Febuary 2012
M9352

Printed in the United States of America

In Memory of

Ann Dunham

"Good morning children," said Ms. Sugar the schoolteacher. "There's going to be a spelling test at the end of the week."

All the cookie crumbs moaned and groaned.

One of the cookie crumbs stayed after school.

"Ms. Sugar," he said, "I have to help my dad on the farm. Can you help me study the words?"

"Of course," said Ms. Sugar. "Can you come to school a little early every day this week?"

"YES," said the excited cookie crumb, "I'll be here bright and early."

The first day of study went very well.

The second day, Ms. Sugar could tell Buster was tired.

13

By the third day, Ms. Sugar and the cookie crumb both looked a little haggard.

When the little cookie crumb got a problem wrong, he got a sour look on his face and rolled his eyes.

"It's no picnic for me either Buster," said Ms. Sugar.

The day of the test came, and all of the students did very well.

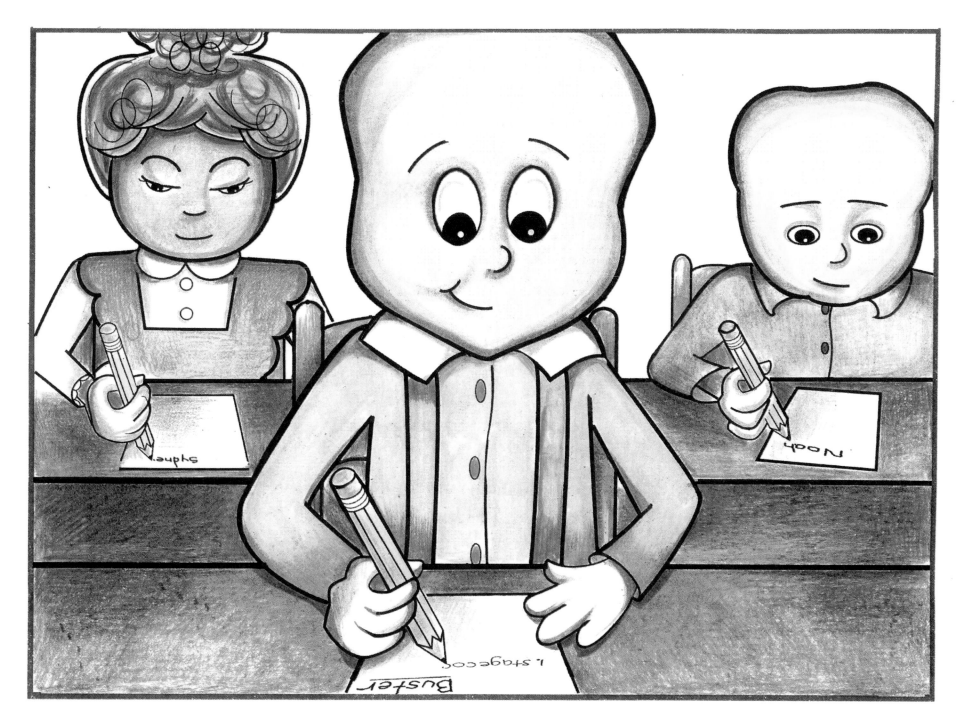

Especially Buster. He was not afraid to ask for help. He got every word correct.

"See what happens if you study and work hard?" asked Ms. Sugar. "You can achieve anything."